Un-TRAINING

MANUAL

By Human Monkey, LLC

ISBN: 978-0-578-08708-5

Copyeditor: Arielle Pollack

Published by Human Monkey, LLC
www.ContinueToEvolve.com

human
monkey

CONTINUE TO EVOLVE

Disclosure

This book is the sole view and perspectives of Human Monkey, LLC. This book is intended to spark the thought process of the reader and to help them find answers in their own journey to a healthier life. Any similarities to any medical practice or psychotherapy are coincidental. It is written to give the reader an understanding that allows them to find their own path in eliminating the chaos created during their childhood.

The information contained in this book is intended to be educational. The author and publisher are in no way liable for any use or misuse of the information.

Acknowledgement

This book is dedicated to all those wanting to...

"CONTINUE TO EVOLVE"

Table of Contents

Conflicting Perceptions

You wouldn't be looking at this book, if you weren't already searching for an answer of some kind. You know things are not the way they should be, but you do not know what it is you are looking for, or where to even search for it.

You have been told that the answers you seek lie inside of you. However, without more information, you know you won't be able to find them.

What *is* happening is that you are unknowingly making your present reality. A reality you yourself are trying to understand and operate in.

This all came about starting the day you were born. You took in your new world tactically. You felt things physically and emotionally well before you had the ability to comprehend things. By not having developed your "thinking" mind yet, your "feeling" mind grew perceptions of its own. It manifested perceptions of your world, your place in it, and of your power over the things in it. Those unseen perceptions have followed you your entire life, creating the reality that your thinking mind is confused by. Your thinking mind finds comfort through the use of coping mechanisms such as control and avoidance.

Now as an adult, you have one brain with two minds, with different perceptions: the conscious *thinking* mind and its perceptions, and the subconscious *feeling* mind with its perceptions.

The answers you are seeking start with *Who am I? Am I self aware? What are my views of my world? What perceptions would my subconscious have that would create my reality?* And, *How did I get those perceptions?* Self-analysis is necessary to reveal the perceptions one has. From there, you have to emotionally relive the events creating those perceptions. It's important to consider every detail so as to retrain your subconscious feeling mind to line up with your thinking mind's perceptions.

So, how does a Human Monkey begin to undo years of training?

Where does a Human Monkey even start?

What does a Human Monkey even look for?

The quickest way to find one's self is to consider the company he or she keeps.

On the following chart, draw a line either higher, on, or below parallel to the centerline, as to what you believe your friend's self-esteem is.

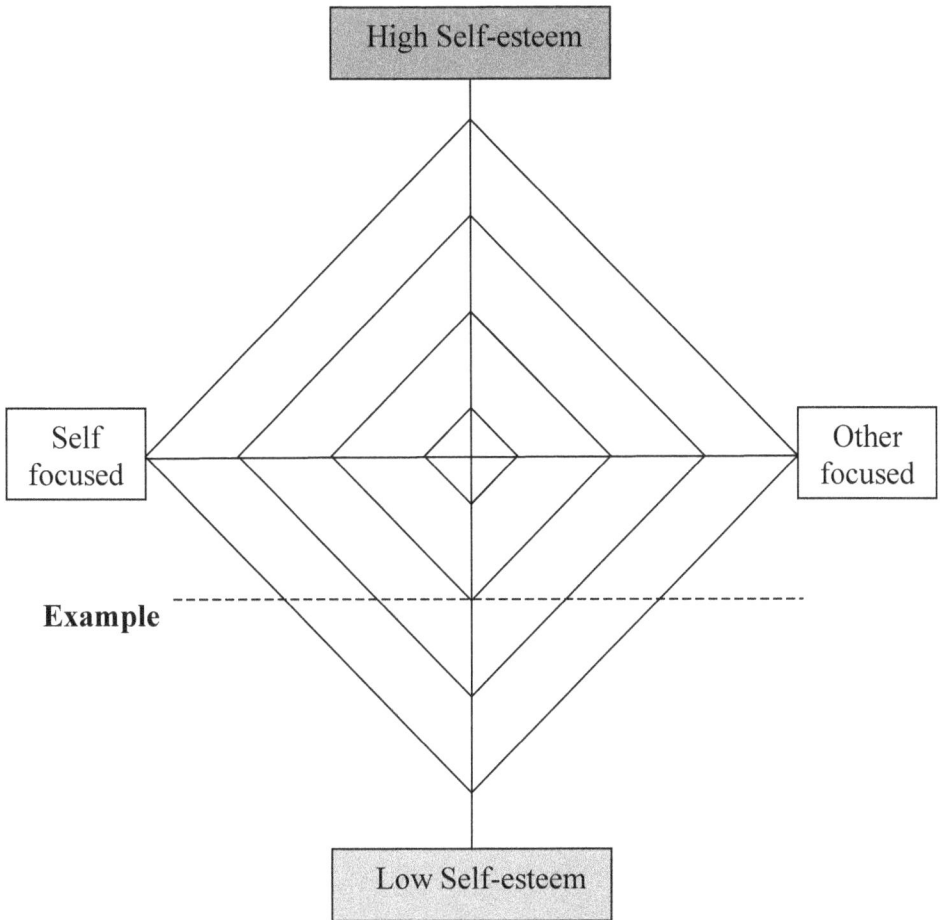

Now, do the same thing again, only this time draw a line left or right of centerline, to the degree you think they are selfish or giving (do they think more of themselves, or are they more concerned as to what other people think or need?).

Do this with three or four of your friends.

Is a picture beginning to emerge?

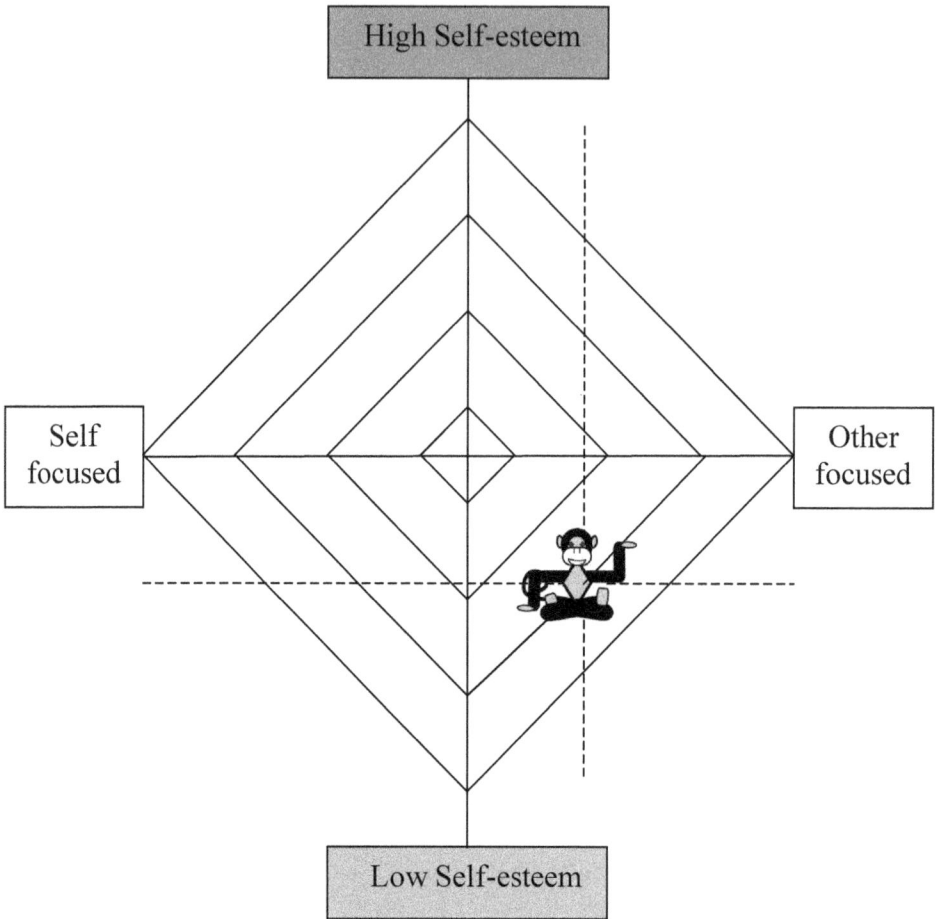

In this example, it appears, that this Human Monkey and his friends have low self-esteem, and are givers (other focused – others are more important than self). Their subconscious feeling mind's perception is what places them there, creating the reality that their thinking mind is attempting to operate in.

Next:

Put a check mark next to the letter that best answers the question as it relates to you.

Some esteem questions:

1) The number of friends I have is.
   A: a lot
   B: above average
   C: average
   D: below average
   E: not many

2) I have a fear of being rejected by others.
   A: never
   B: rarely
   C: sometimes
   D: usually
   E: always

3) I am comfortable trying new things.
   A: always
   B: usually
   C: sometimes
   D: rarely
   E: never

4) I forgive myself for making mistakes.
   A: always
   B: usually
   C: sometimes
   D: rarely
   E: never

Now:

Some self/other focus questions:

1) I'm concerned what others think of me.
   A: never
   B: rarely
   C: sometimes
   D: usually
   E: always

2) Do you feel your needs are more important to you, than the needs of others?
   A: always
   B: usually
   C: sometimes
   D: rarely
   E: never

3) I feel I have a strong need for approval and praise.
   A: never
   B: rarely
   C: sometimes
   D: usually
   E: always

4) I second-guess myself.
   A: never
   B: rarely
   C: sometimes
   D: usually
   E: always

In the first part you plotted your friends. Well congratulations, you found yourself! Human Monkeys *are* pack animals; birds of a feather flock together. We group ourselves with people of similar interest, IQ, and self-esteem. We find comfort through the protection of being with our own herd. It helps to ensure our survival.

By answering the questions in the second part, you are further verifying your location on the chart.

Esteem questions, if you primarily answered A or B, you are above the centerline, C, on the centerline, and D or E, below the centerline.

Self/other focus questions, if you answered A or B you are left of the centerline, C, on the centerline, and D or E, right of the centerline.

Now that we are getting a clearer picture of our own position, let us continue to move on to how we undo all the false training we unknowingly learned in childhood.

The first step in un-training the Human Monkey animal is to understand how it was originally trained.

The young human animal that has yet to develop a conscious reasoning mind with an experience database from which to draw upon is vulnerable to lies and misinformation. This is when the confusion first begins. The child can only react from his or her emotional feeling mind.

For example, imagine a family of Human Monkeys on vacation. For fun, the parent tells the child to place their hand on top of the glass aquarium, above an alligator, so that in the photo the child appears to be petting the alligator.

The child, however, is terrified to pose so closely to the alligator. So, who is this event really about, the parent or the child?

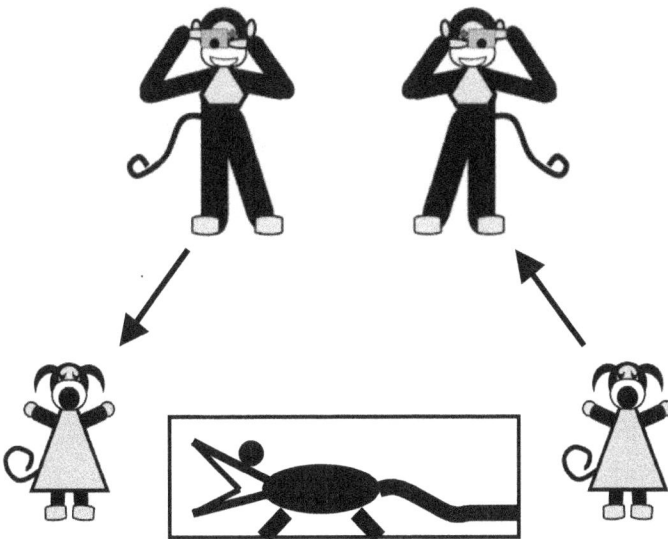

Or, for example, a Human Monkey parent is angry with its child for getting failing grades in school. The parent, in anger, breaks the guitar they had given the child as a Christmas present. What power game is being played? Is this about the child failing in school, or about the parent's need of control over the child? So, once again, who is this event really about, the parent or the child?

In a different example, the Human Monkey parent idolizes their child, as if they can do no wrong. The family is out shopping and the child becomes demanding. The child knows no boundaries, and has been taught that everyone is there solely for its needs. Everything is "all about" it. The parent does not correct this behavior.

All of the confusion is created when the adults responsible for the child's wellbeing send conflicting messages. This occurs when the actions, words, or both are supposed to be about the child's betterment, but are actually about the adult's needs. This causes unconscious confusion for the child as it is learning how to survive in its environment. This confusion will create fear. Ultimately these fears may lead to insecurities.

These subtle, but confusing behaviors sink deep into the developing child's subconscious feeling mind, and begin to give the young Human Monkey animal an unconscious perception of itself. These unconsciously felt perceptions, buried deep within your subconscious, are what you will need to fully comprehend to be able to "un-train" yourself.

These "skewed" perceptions can be charted by looking at the Human Monkey's self-esteem and self-focus.

These false perceptions are the foundation of the young animal's mind. The confused young Human Monkey, instead of being healthy and centered, having subconsciously consumed its skewed perception of itself is off-center. That off-center unconscious perception can be seen and plotted.

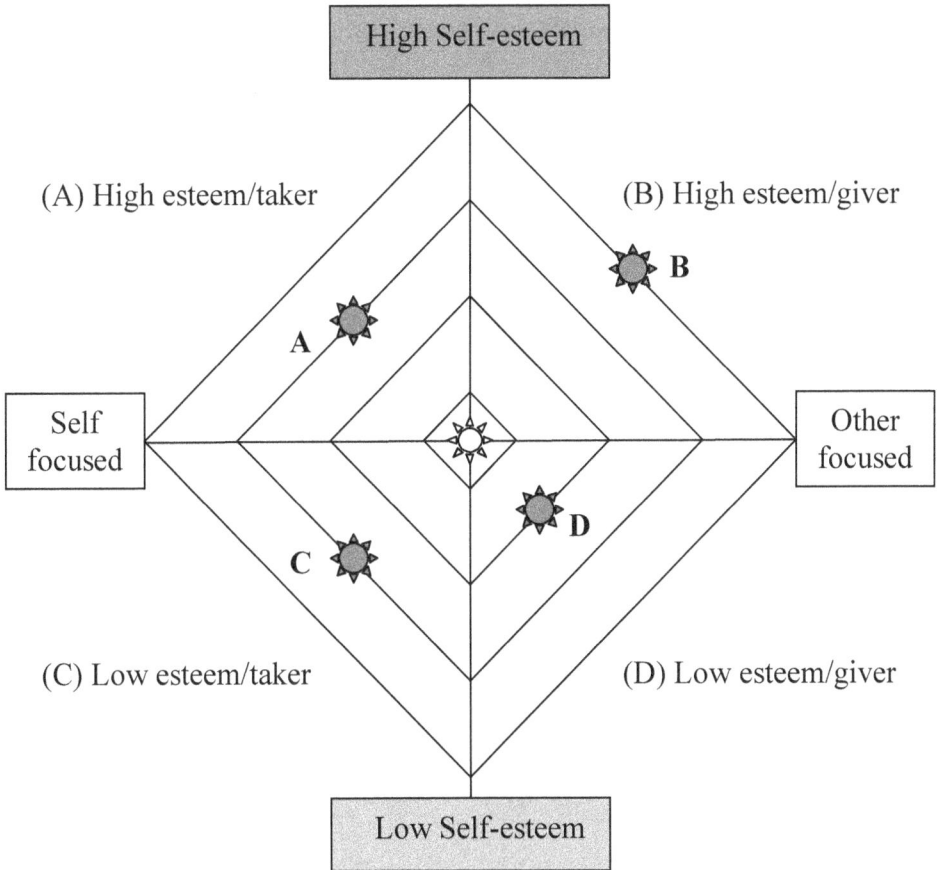

High Self-esteem

(A) High esteem/taker

(B) High esteem/giver

B

A

Self focused

Other focused

D

C

(C) Low esteem/taker

(D) Low esteem/giver

Low Self-esteem

This deep subconscious perception of self hardens with age. Unaware of the off-center state even believing that they are centered more confusion will be created as the Human Monkey animal ages! This causes it to move even farther away from a life of centeredness.

This confusion will create more subconscious fear and insecurities that will also have to be processed and comforted.

The insecurities are rooted so deep in the subconscious they become needs. Needs that are as important to the mind as oxygen! As the young logical mind is developing, it can only comfort those needs through the development of coping mechanisms such as control, avoidance, passive aggression, and so forth.

Through the use of these coping mechanisms, personalities will begin to form. Once again, because of the underlying foundation, we can easily plot all the different personalities.

Unstable Foundation

Self focused	High Self-esteem	Other focused
Narcissistic side of chart		Victim role side of chart

Superiority complex

Know it all | Righteous

Tease | Pacifist

Egotist | 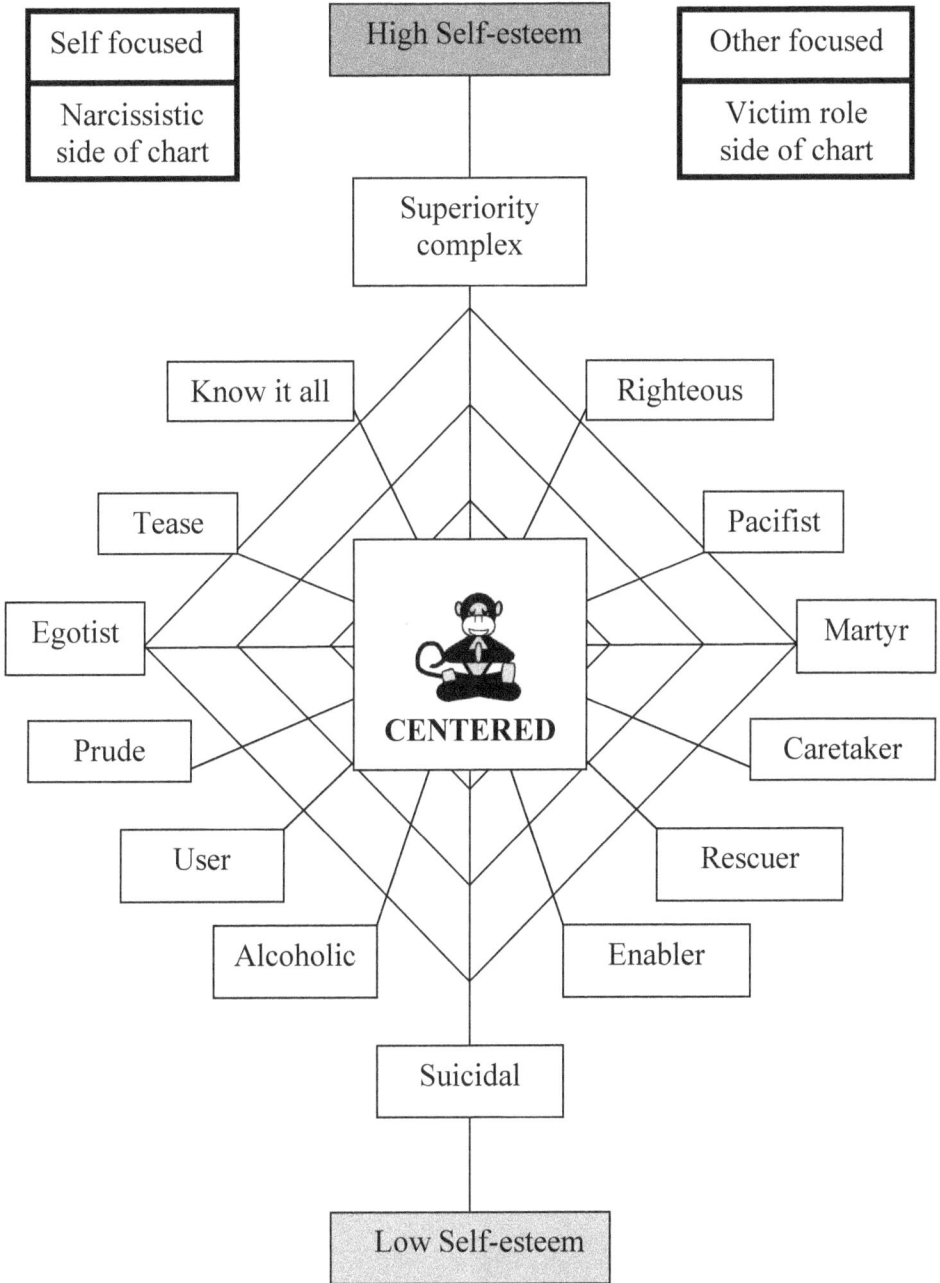 | Martyr

CENTERED

Prude | Caretaker

User | Rescuer

Alcoholic | Enabler

Suicidal

Low Self-esteem

The driving force behind the desire to be in a relationship is the need to breed that evolved; it's the continuing of a species to produce Human Monkey offspring. That offspring, which in turn, will learn confusing ways of surviving its environment, primarily influenced by its parents. The cycle will continue on and on.

Since our developing Human Monkey animal has so much confusion, which has led to many needs it will seek out a mating partner to aid in meeting those needs. Someone with the same level of self-esteem, and with either the same or opposite self focus, thus developing a need-based relationship. A relationship where each partner will look to get his or her happiness from the other partner, by getting his or her needs met.

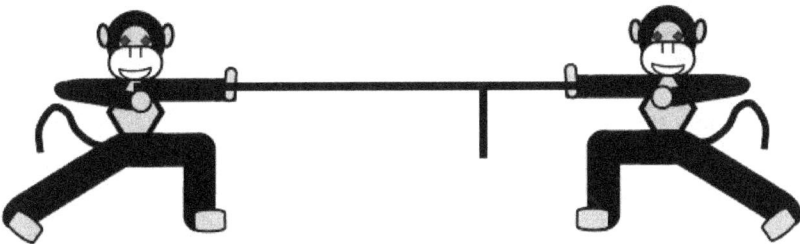

* Need-based: the unseen tug-of-war to get unknown needs met.

So from birth, which overall message did the Human Monkey child learn to believe that its initial survival was dependent on?

"It is about me" | Or | "It is about them"

Then, it would become either…

"A Taker" | Or | "A Giver"

His or her relationships will be:

"About me"

"About them"

And he or she will find:

"Attention from others gives it happiness"

"It get happiness by giving to others"

This in return will give it:

"A feeling of being valued, i.e. important"

"A sense of having value, of being needed"

These need based relationships can also be plotted.

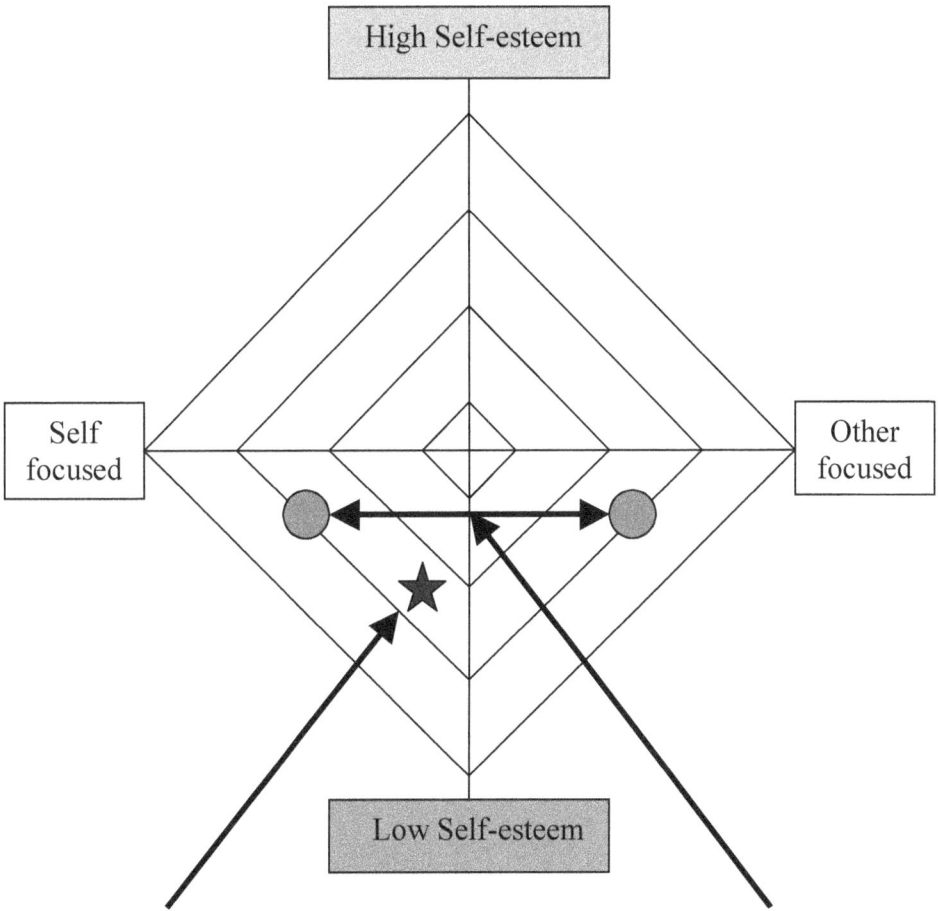

So-called "Healthy" relationship   **"Co-dependent" relationship**

By comparing this relationship chart with the personality chart, you can begin to see how a need-based relationship feels right. By balancing out each other, each feel centered. Your goal is to find "centeredness" alone, by removing the subconscious confusion you unknowingly learned in your childhood.

The so-called healthy relationship is one that is matched in three arenas. Both partners are in same quadrant having the same esteem, give-take, and interest, in other words, they think they have found their soul mate! Other criteria such as physical attraction, habits, religious beliefs, and financial attitudes will further increase that consensus. In reality, both partners are not centered, only matched. They still need to be in a relationship.

The co-dependant relationship is where the partner mirrors you in interest and self-esteem, and where opposites attract (selfish/selfless). These people, being of the same self-esteem level, balance each other out. The needs of the other, the give and take being met, will create the illusion of fulfillment, i.e., true love. Couples believe they have found balance, i.e., you complete me! Both esteems will initially rise with "romantic love." However, being co-dependent the coping mechanisms will begin to push them apart. If the bond breaks, they will move even farther from center.

Guilt is one of the primary tools the mind uses to try to keep the other partner in the desired place. Trying to maintain the believed balance, so they can get their needs met.

Coping mechanisms are the actions, i.e. manipulations that attempt to create the guilt. While blame is the self defense mechanism, the mind uses in its attempt to not feel the guilt.

Coping mechanisms can be broken down into the two categories. However, both givers and takers will use all to varying degrees in order to get needs met.

> 1) Givers (Other-focused/Selfless) will use:
>> A: Control - to fix or fulfill, to eliminate a problem
>> B: Righteousness - to degrade others
>> C: Self pity - to get someone to feel sorry for them

> 2) Takers (Self-focused/Selfish) will use:
>> A: Passive aggressions - to equalize
>> B: Avoidance - to negate, other person is not important
>> C: Martyr - to show that they're better than the other
>> D: People pleasing - to avoid conflict

Your roadmap: "CONTINUE TO EVOLVE"

1) Becoming aware
2) Understanding the timeline
3) Comprehending your dreams
4) Modifying behavior
5) What to expect
6) Loving yourself

The key is education getting the facts.

1) Becoming aware:

The first step is to become aware, start searching, ask why, why, why! At the beginning, this will be very difficult. Remember, we are mostly emotional beings. This attempt to look at ourselves honestly will be met with great resistance. On the deepest of levels, your mind knows once you pull on the thread to unravel things you are opening Pandora's box! This huge unknown and seemingly overwhelming task will be met with fear. Your mind, being mostly emotional, is made up of reacting and fear. It will want to choose to stay safely living in denial - it will justify, and anything else, to avoid opening that box. The questions equal great fear, equating to great pain, even to the point of possibly even ending in death! Your mind will use every tool (trick) to prevent you from pulling that string. It will be all right; you have a roadmap.

Go ahead and truthfully look at your friends. What do you really think of them? Write down what you think, and plot them on the self-esteem/focus chart. Look close, remember, that's you too!

If you are with them, then you have the same esteem with similar dysfunctions. Take an honest look at yourself, accept it, and start your journey to a healthier life.

Now with a starting point...

2) Understanding the timeline:

Instead of paying thousands of dollars, and going to someone to have them keep asking, "So, how did you feel about that?" or "How did that make you feel?" and spending a lifetime buying them a new house, just do it for yourself. Ask yourself those same questions: why, what, how.

It will be very difficult staying the course. The mind will take the medicine, i.e. facing the truth, to the point where the emotional pain stops. It's continuing to search for the answers even after the pain quits, which is daunting.

This is what can happen to a substance abuser. They get the control over their addiction and the pain stops; the mind believes it has found the answer. Now having control, they choose to quit searching for more answers. Remember, the mind equates pain to eventual death, so it's extremely hard to keep pulling up painful memories to purge the subconscious. One is going against its own innate, millions of years old instinct of basic survival - *avoid pain!* It's like taking antibiotics: one must keep taking the drugs even after they feel well. Continue to peel back the layers, all the way back to the day you were born. Re-trace every event and heal. Allow your mind to relive each experience. You visually consume it emotionally into your feeling mind without the filter of logic being unable to understand all the facts. You must re-live events emotionally. Allow yourself to feel everything. If angry, punch a pillow. When sad, step in the shower and wail. To weep is a subconscious release; to cry is a conscious relief.

Remember, this time you can re-write the event with the truth of what really occurred with the benefit of being older, having a knowledge base and experience to pull from.

A good rule of thumb to use is 10 percent of your age. If you are thirty years old, your "homework" will take around three years to complete. The mind has to retrieve data, relive that data, delete data, and re-install data all emotionally for every event of your life where what you consumed wasn't the reality at all. The only way to gauge if or where one needs to work is to compare where there is a disagreement between what you logically think and what you are physically doing or seeing. If there is, it's a need still attempting to be met!

Remember, the focus isn't on the addiction (alcohol, drugs, etc.) it's on the real root cause. What happened in your childhood environment that later in life would create such confusion that the mind would need the substance to comfort it? Unravel the pain. Remember, alcohol numbs the pain like aspirin does with physical pain. It's not just a disease; it's an overuse of self-medicating. Dig deep and learn what is causing you the pain.

Each painful event will require certain steps to be completed. You will need to go through the following steps for each event:

1) Denial - shock, disbelief, etc.
2) Grief - sadness as the magnitude of loss sinks in.
3) Anger - as the vast confusion sets in from the realization that it didn't need to happen.
4) Acceptance - facts allow the mind to comprehend all the data. The mind realizes how the numbers added up, and that there was no other possible outcome.

In the past, your mind may have stopped at level three many times without having all the data. You may have buried that anger without comprehending; this is what is known as suppressed anger.

The more confusing events you have experienced, the more suppressed anger you have. This anger expresses itself externally as rage, and depression when turned inward. As time goes by the anger (confusion emotionally expressed) becomes buried under layers and layers of new day-to-day data without ever getting an answer. It will become like a "boil" lying there like a time bomb. Every so often, a life event will come along that pokes at that hidden boil causing it to seep pus, i.e., emotional pain created by years of not being resolved. That boil will continue to cause you problems if you do not go in, pull back the layers, lance that boil, and relieve the confusing event that created it. Then, like a physical wound, it too can emotionally heal. Being both comprehended consciously and subconsciously.

Anger is the emotional response created by your own confusion. This means anger *is* always at ones self! So, when you think that someone is causing you anger, remember, you are confused - that is what is making you angry. It's your issue to resolve by finding your answers to your confusion. They have done nothing! You are the one not understanding things.

Lets review once again how you were trained.

By messages:

word + action = message

Your childhood confusion was created by conflicting messages.

Let's take a closer look at how we receive mixed messages as children, accepting them as reality without our ability to reason.

Truths

Word + Action

"I love you" Hug

| Left hemisphere
Language/Math
Reasons…
Logical mind
Conscience | Right hemisphere
Visual/Images
"Mind photos"
Intuitive / led by feelings
Reacts
Emotional mind
Subconscious |

And, now….

Lies

Word + Action

"I love you" Hit

| Left hemisphere
Language/Math
Reasons…
Logical mind
Conscience | Right hemisphere
Visual/Images
"Mind photos"
Intuitive / led by feelings
Reacts
Emotional mind
Subconscious |
| It is the lie from the person saying it. (Non-fact) | It is the truth from the person doing the action. |

By balancing the truth and lies the child experiences, the individual arrives at its believed place on the self-esteem/focus chart.

Because your logical conscience thinking mind is just a few million years old, and your emotional subconscious feeling mind is millions of years old, you, the Human Monkey animal, will still learn like all other mammals. Your brain tissue takes in many stimuli from many different nerve endings, stores, and defrags the data. The majority of data you obtain is through visual, i.e., seen.

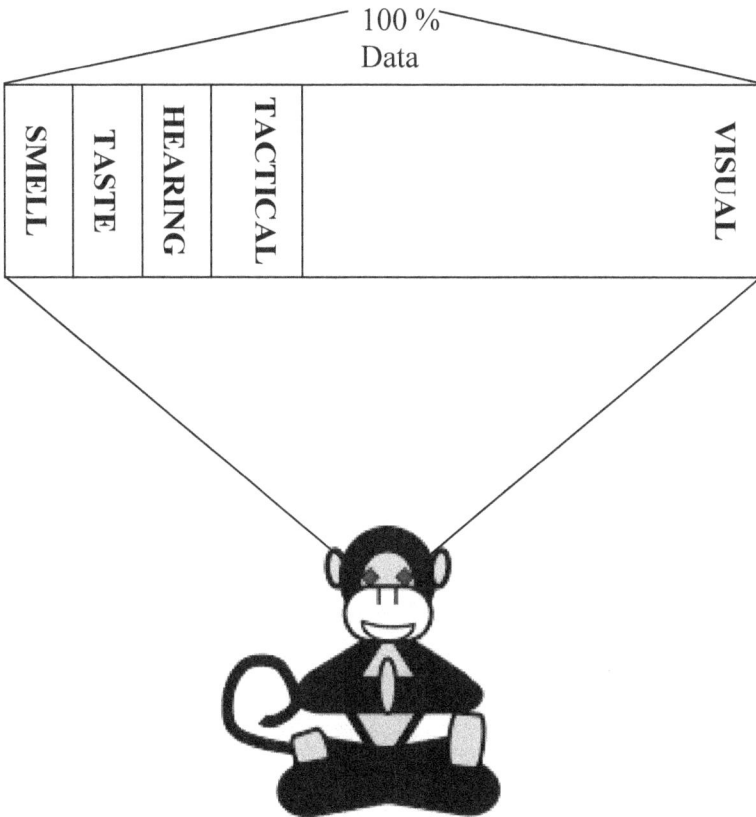

100 %
Data

| SMELL | TASTE | HEARING | TACTICAL | | VISUAL |

Without the filter of logic, the child will interpret what it sees with the amount of stored data. The subconscious will begin interpreting its place, the societal pecking order, and what is needed to continue to survive. It balances out what works and doesn't, then imprints it on the subconscious to operate from. Right, or wrong!

This is why it is important to begin to understand your dreams. Your subconscious is communicating its thoughts back to your conscious as you awake through visual communication. It is the reverse of how it was taken in.

3) Comprehending your dreams:

Water is your subconscious. How deep is it? The deeper the water, the greater the homework! The depth of the water is equal to the distance between your conscious and your subconscious being aligned, i.e. having the same perceptions. Your subconscious "sees" you and the world far differently than you think.

A House/home is your view of you (could be houseboat, etc). Is it big and open, or is it small with no windows?

A Rock is your perception of your power. It is the amount of control you have over your life versus outside factors. Example: A small stone being tossed about by waves, or a boulder holding steady.

Rising means an answer is coming, floating up from your subconscious to your conscious.

Naked, either you or them, is the amount of one's vulnerability determined by the amount of clothes one is wearing.

Falling is a loss of control.

In the morning, lie there in bed and ease the dream from your subconscious to your conscious. Allow yourself to lie there and fully hold the information in your awakening conscious mind.

Analyze it throughout the day, and ask yourself what it meant. You took in events visually as a child, so the only way the subconscious can give the information back is visually through your dreams.

Even though we all have common dreams, this doesn't mean yours will be the same. Remember, the dream came from you, only you know what it means. Ask yourself during the day for the answer, and it will pop into your head. After all, it's your dream!

Learn to use your dreams as the medium between your two minds.

Learn to understand what the dreams are telling you about your own self-esteem. How you view yourself and the world, from the real you, the driving force behind your reality - your subconscious.

See how your subconscious is coming into alignment with your conscious as you do your homework, and clean out the emotionally consumed visually imprinted lies.

With a little practice, you will learn the art of deciphering. You will know instinctively if what your conscious mind thinks is in agreement with your subconscious. If it isn't, you will "feel" it in the form of a gut feeling.

Dreams come from three things:

1) Physical aliments and pain while you're asleep, for example, lying uncomfortably on your arm.
2) Items it is defragging, the things you have seen during the day. It is deciding what to keep or delete (all learning occurs while you sleep).
3) Your subconscious perceptions of yourself or your environment.

You will be shown separately, or a combination of up to all three at once, thus the weirdness of dreams. As you awake, and you lie there between conscious and subconscious, build the habit of concentrating on the dream. Train yourself to remember the dream as you come into full consciousness.

Then you simply have to ask yourself, what am I showing myself? What part of the dream meant what? Was it just defragging, was I seeing the previous day's events? Or, was it showing me my true self?

Keep asking your mind: "What are you showing me?"

Your brain as you awake:

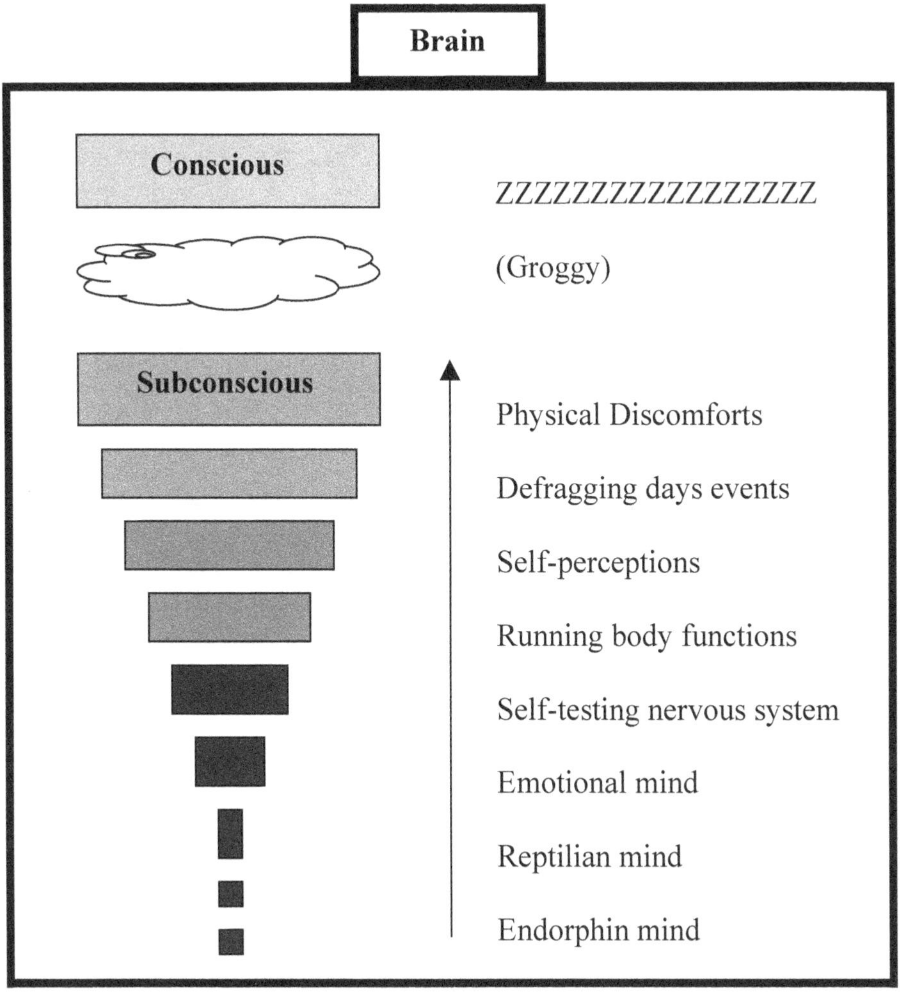

Brain

| Conscious | ZZZZZZZZZZZZZZZZZZ |

(Groggy)

| Subconscious |

Physical Discomforts

Defragging days events

Self-perceptions

Running body functions

Self-testing nervous system

Emotional mind

Reptilian mind

Endorphin mind

* The Human Monkey's subconscious has evolved to be nine layers deep.

4) Modifying behavior:

Retraining yourself, practice doing what you say.

Action match words = message.

Messages, messages, messages!

Simplify things in your life; learn what needs you are trying to meet. Don't feed them; continue to understand what is driving them.

De-clutter your life as much as possible. The only real needs are food, water, clothing, and shelter. After learning who you really are, what emotional needs you were attempting to meet, then you can add in the wants for yourself.

Less external stuff means less chance of internal confusion.

Be good to yourself: Love (value) yourself and forgive (understand) yourself. Give yourself the love and the information, that as a child, you would have liked to have received.

Don't forget to reward you, the Human Monkey, when you've made progress, it helps to continue the desire for further self-awareness and self-growth.

Constant positive re-enforcement!

Your goal:

To always send positive messages to and from self and to others!

Word	
Action	→ Message

Word	
Action	→ Message

Word	
Action	→ Message

Word	
Action	→ Message

Word	
Action	→ Message

Word	
Action	→ Message

The real message

Cumulative

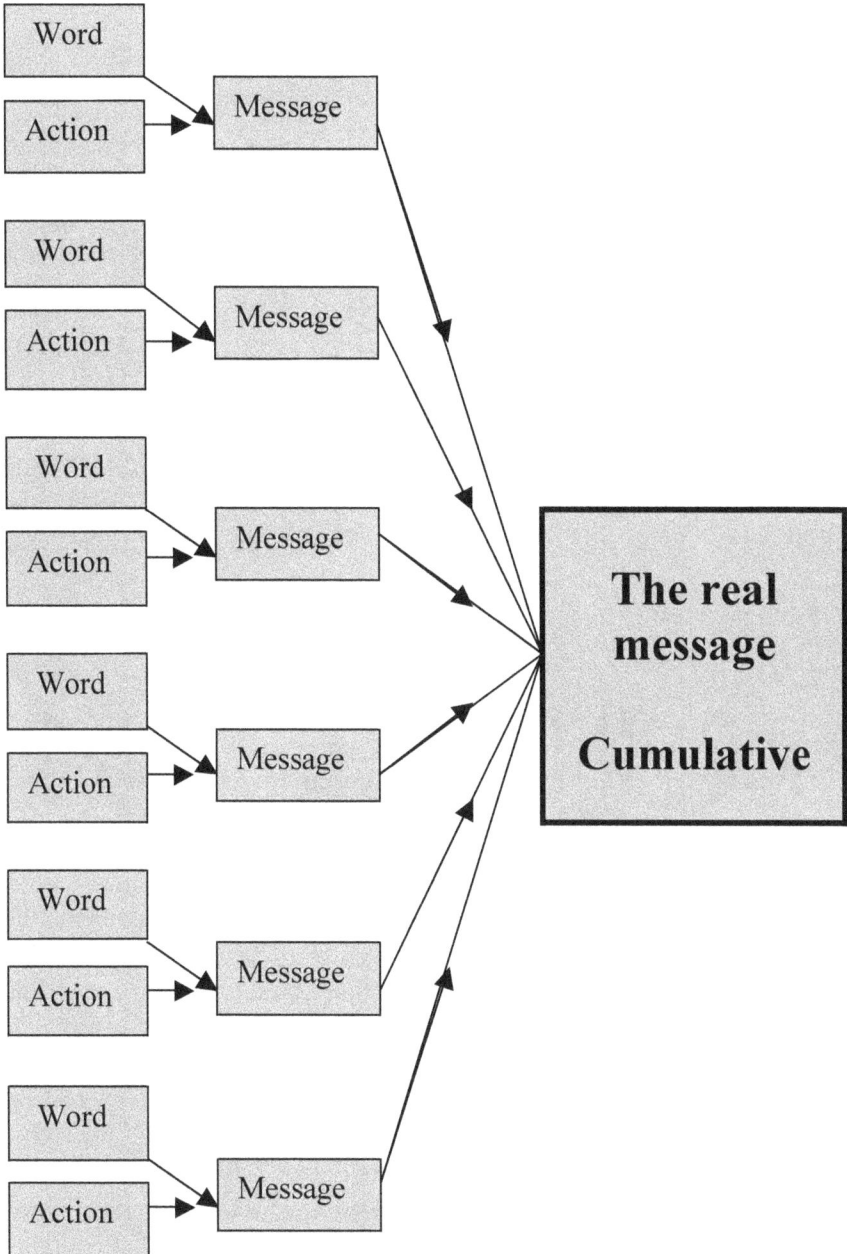

The ultimate message is that you are loved, which means you have value! All words and messages need to be the facts, i.e., the truth. Reality requires the actions to be the same as the words.

5) What to expect:

It's going to be a rollercoaster ride!

As you learn and comprehend something, the mind will be joyful. Then as you gain ground and the mind sees there is more territory, and what you've previously learned sinks in, you will be depressed. You will also be experiencing plateaus and setbacks.

Some days you will feel as if you take two steps forward and one back. Remember, it's one small step after another.

This is what your emotional ride is going to feel like as you learn and correlate data. Feelings of joy, then periods of sadness, and then finally anger. You will repeat this over and over, as you learn and grow.

There is going to be a lot of confusion while the mind chews on new data, and learns to view things differently. You'll have trouble understanding things. As you change, love yourself more, and feel better, the people around you will be hostile towards you.

This is because you are changing, and it is messing with their comfort zone. They must change too, or put you back into the role they have known you in for years. People will subconsciously be attempting to put you back in that role. This will cause conflict between you and them. They will not see what you see.

You may begin to outgrow friends, family and loved ones. They will live in denial and stay safely shackled in their dysfunctional world, as you begin to see the real behaviors for what they are. Subconscious needs trying to be met.

You will begin to see the world completely different. And, see people for who they are, not what their logical mind is trying to portray. You will see how you are undoing the victim or narcissistic mentality of your own existence. You will realize the things you were doing were all fear driven. And, you will begin to enjoy a simpler life. You will understand that there has never been anywhere to get to, even though you have been racing to get there all your life.

It took time to get off track; it will take time to correct and to heal. It will take around ten percent of your lifetime thus far!

6) Loving yourself:

If you are doing things that logically are not good for you, such as drinking, smoking, etc. then you are not valuing yourself. Be kind, and treat yourself as you would if you were the parent of yourself. How would you like to have been treated as a child? Now, do it that way!

The number one thing you can do for yourself is to get regular sleep. The Human Monkey animal evolved to have regular sleep. This regulates all else.

Diet is next, remember you are a primate, eat like one. Graze when at all possible; eat small amounts many times a day. Only eat when you are hungry. Try to eat similar to what a primate would, i.e. earth to mouth. The less steps in-between the better. Stay away as much as possible from breads, unless they are sprouted grain, and stay away from as many processed foods as possible. Stick to a diet that is mostly, water, vegetable, fruits, nuts, berries, and proteins. However, don't forget to reward yourself with the occasional treat!

Do exercises regularly. Like dieting, exercise a few minutes here and there throughout the day. The best and easiest exercise to do is what you evolved to do, walk. You stood upright, so you could walk. Do exercises that are fun. Playing in the animal kingdom sharpens skills. So, go play, and get healthy while having fun!

Groom yourself regularly; healthy animals maintain and even preen themselves.

Clean and organize your nest (home/living area); healthy animals maintain their nest/den, or abandon it!

Remember, you're an evolved mammal, so sleep, eat, play, groom!

* As always, consult your doctor before making changes in your diet, or exercise routine!

Review

Just as your ancestors once lived primarily in their emotional "feeling" mind, reacting, you must make the conscious decision to live primarily in your logical "thinking" mind and act. Remove the bad data, so the emotional mind won't want to react, and stop living in denial.

In order to just be, you must have quietness of the soul, i.e., the mind. You must completely rid it of all confusion!

Once you have done *all* of your homework - cleaned out the pus from the consumed boils of your subconscious - retrained your subconscious to align with your conscious, and began "doing as you say" and "being the person you want to be," no meditating or soul searching will ever be needed again. Answering all of your questions leaves your mind endlessly quiet and content - blissful!

Never stop asking the question why, until there are no more whys. This will take time, possibly many, many years, depending on your age. There is no short cut, no quick fix, and no trick.

You must make actions equal words. If you cannot, then you must keep searching, and keep asking the why questions until you have unraveled and removed the confusion that is creating the insecurity that is driving the action.

Learn to decipher your dreams to understand what your subconscious thinks of you and is telling you. Then go through the four steps of grief, remove the boil, heal, and rewrite the experience using only the facts. Then through actions fully retrain the subconscious to align with your conscious.

Then your life will be full of lasting joy coming from your subconscious, allowing your conscious to feel happiness and sadness as appropriate.

Now, let's do a quick review what we've learned:

We psychologically move as we age, but falsely believe we are growing centered. Confidence (conscious) is not esteem (subconscious). We are what we taught ourselves to be. Our self-esteem, values, selfishness, and habits are all emotionally learned while we are surviving and attempting to logically understand what happens around us. The problem is that falsehoods become deeply imprinted before we can even comprehend what it is we are learning.

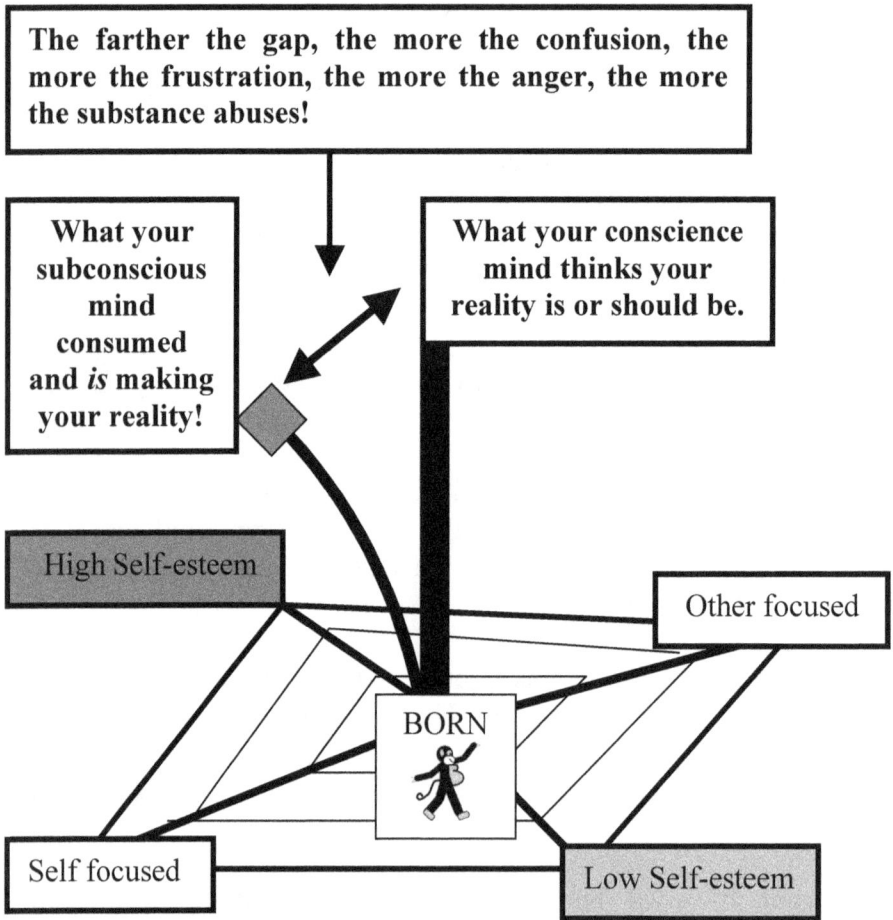

The farther the gap, the more the confusion, the more the frustration, the more the anger, the more the substance abuses!

What your subconscious mind consumed and *is* making your reality!

What your conscience mind thinks your reality is or should be.

High Self-esteem

Other focused

BORN

Self focused

Low Self-esteem

* The length of the curve is the age of the individual.

**   ◇   Each person believes they are centered.

That consumed subconscious confusion unknowingly places you somewhere on the self-esteem/focus chart (the aerial view of our psychological movement).

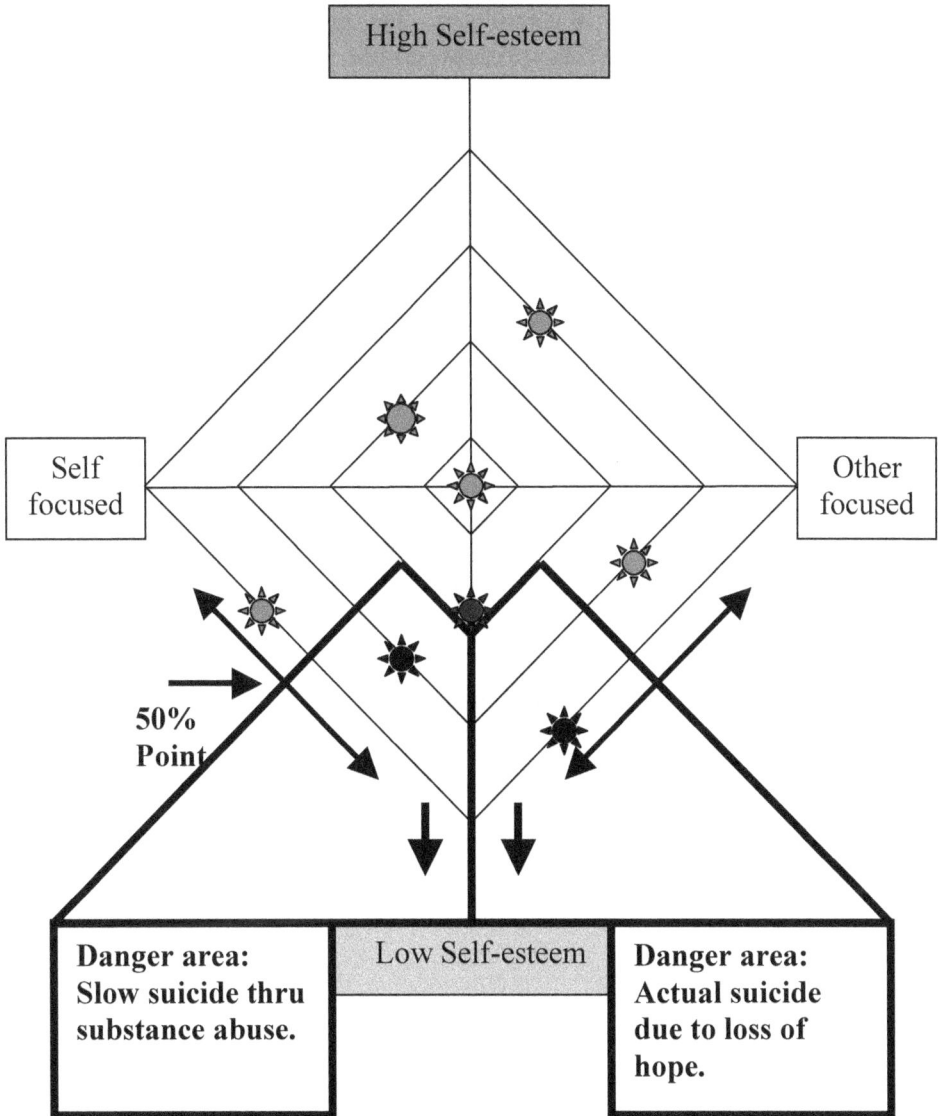

High Self-esteem

Self focused

Other focused

50% Point

Danger area: Slow suicide thru substance abuse.

Low Self-esteem

Danger area: Actual suicide due to loss of hope.

* Survival: the most important requirements in a survival situation are mental attitude and the will to live. Both of these are lost when the confusion of the mind places a person into one of the "danger areas."

Now that we know where our subconscious training unknowingly placed us, we will need to logically trace back all of the facts leading to getting there. All the way back to our birth, seeing and comprehending all of the facts that would have created those initial subconscious perceptions of ourselves, the ones we constructed our life upon, which is creating our present reality.

Your conscience mind learns logically, your subconscious mind learns tactically through feeling things physically and emotionally. Your evolved Human Monkey brain learns through four steps: rote, correlating, understanding, and then application. Repeated application allows for a stronger building block, which allows more blocks to be added, equaling more growth and understanding.

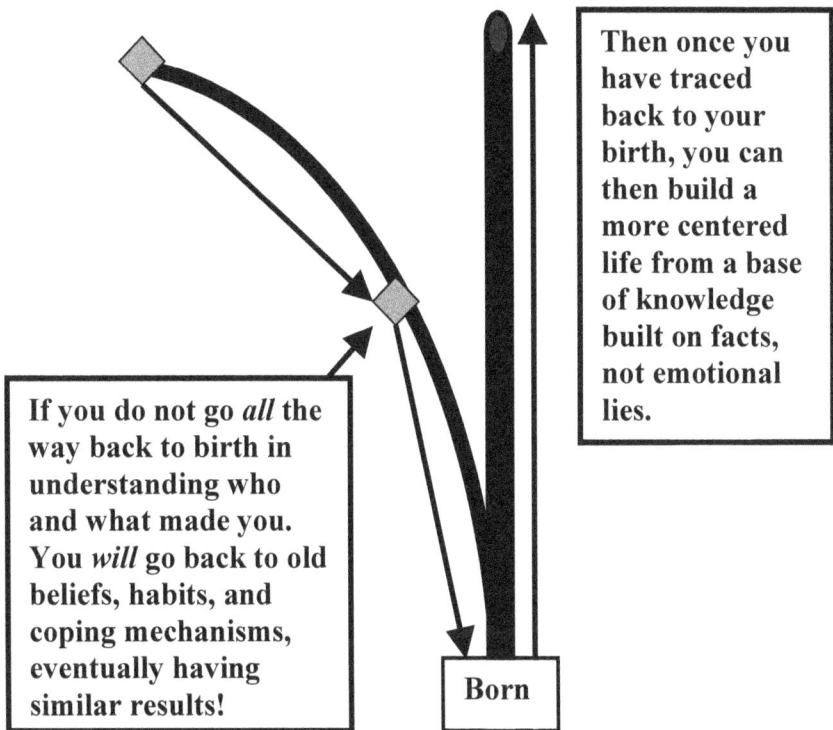

Then once you have traced back to your birth, you can then build a more centered life from a base of knowledge built on facts, not emotional lies.

If you do not go *all* the way back to birth in understanding who and what made you. You *will* go back to old beliefs, habits, and coping mechanisms, eventually having similar results!

Born

"CONTINUE TO EVOLVE"

Highlights to remember:

1) We learn things emotionally well before having a logical capacity to understand what it is we are learning.
2) This unknowingly gives us our self-esteem and self-focus.
3) Any confusion creates fears and insecurities, which leads to needs.
4) We unconsciously develop coping mechanisms in an attempt to meet those needs.
5) Those needs cause us to seek out need-based relationships.

To "CONTINUE TO EVOLVE"

1) Look at your friends and mate, and see your real self-esteem, and self-focus.
2) Start mentally retracing steps that you think would have led to you being where you are.
3) Emotionally feel, and in your mind visually relive those events. Feeling every detail!
4) Emotionally release the feelings that are brought up.
5) Replace those thoughts with the reality of what occurred, not what you felt at the time it occurred.
6) Monitor yourself through your dreams, it's your subconscious visually telling you what's going on underneath.
7) Purposely show yourself through your actions that you love (value) you!
8) Continue sending messages (words = actions) of value to yourself and others. Repetition builds habits!
9) Learn to see when your actions are really about yourself, or someone else's actions are truly about themselves, when you or they say otherwise. This helps you to stay and live in reality, not the projected reality that created all the confusion in the first place!

Now, begin plotting and tracking your progress as you un-train yourself, and build a healthier you!

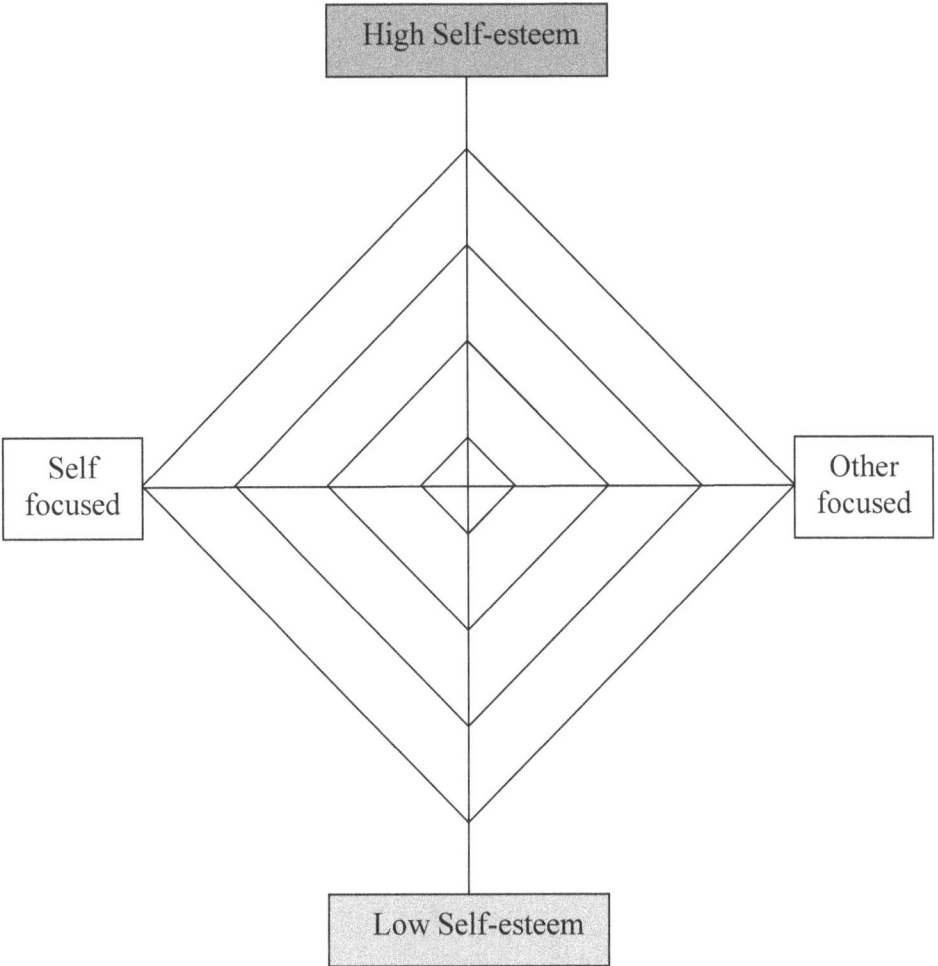

Notes to self:

_____

_____

_____

_____

_____

_____

_____